Golden Honey

ERICA VARELA / MAGESOUL PUBLISHING
PO BOX 580019
BRONX, NY 10458
WWW.MAGESOUL.COM

PUBLISHER'S NOTE: THIS IS A WORK OF FICTION. NAMES, CHARACTERS, PLACES, AND INCIDENTS ARE A PRODUCT OF THE AUTHOR'S IMAGINATION. LOCALES AND PUBLIC NAMES ARE SOMETIMES USED FOR ATMOSPHERIC PURPOSES. ANY RESEMBLANCE TO ACTUAL PEOPLE, LIVING OR DEAD, OR TO BUSINESSES, COMPANIES, EVENTS, INSTITUTIONS, OR LOCALES IS COMPLETELY COINCIDENTAL.

EDITED BY **ZEESHAN ABID** (FIVERR/ZNAMIDE)
COVER ARTWORK FROM **SHUTTERSTOCK**

BULK PURCHASES FROM MAGESOUL PUBLISHING ARE AVAILABLE WITH DISCOUNTS.

GOLDEN HONEY / ERICA VARELA – 2ND ED.
ISBN 9780998040363

Golden Honey
Erica Varela

I would like to dedicate *Golden Honey* to all those who have had to battle with a mental Illness, for their families, loved ones and friends.

I, as a manic depressive, am here to share my stories on love, family, losing friends, and having been institutionalized—all through poetry and my daily life.

For any and everyone who is going through this ache with our loved ones, may we stay strong. Humankind, to see with fresh eyes, know that we are just like you, and we all deserve to be and feel equal.

Together we can remove this stigma that holds us in cages,

Erica Varela

when we all deserve to *fly*.

Golden Honey

Poems by: Erica Varela

Contents

Telling the Story

Closing this book before it begins
would be a tragedy, so we keep re-
reading
our lines, repeating what we know is
right.

When I've fallen close to the ground
you keep me floating. How long 'til
you
give in? My heart can't emerge from
below
the ground if you don't fight for new
soil.

Mud dries, pages loosen.
This story starts with <u>you</u> and <u>me</u>.

Dark Blue

How deep the ocean—may it swallow
me
whole, for I am of thirst.

Scotland

As haunted below, I offer
my soul, for the skies above
once again have left me
to defend on my own.

A cliff above your violent waves
to keep me breathless and blue.

I've become a haunted memory—
a part of you.

Come, ocean tides, sweep me under
your
breathless waves of delight.

Closer

I get in a mood, get shy,
confused, when my thoughts
are of you. But it's only
when I'm with you
that I feel free.
It's in the way
you comfort me.
And the way
our bodies meet perfectly.

Wasn't,
looking for love, not this
soon. I'm falling fast but
I don't mind
landing today.
I wouldn't want it
any other way.

Bouquet

She smelled of sweet flowers
wilted over.
Her family home, surrounded: white
picket families

broken with splinters.

Sparsely—
in the hearts she gathers.

Full bloom.

Explosive Hearts

In your room, sunlight
shines bright through the shades.
We lie and watch the birds
flock by; with our morning daydreams.

That's what we do,
we lie in your bed,
all day.

In grey sheets; our scents linger.

Heart Removal

A distant known stranger, voice to
remember.
Spoken with a sweet hello,
she told me a story,
waiting in line,
order-ready.

I told her she reminded me of a song
that wasn't pretty.
When she asked why,
I told her, I always knew
You'd be the one sitting delectable.

After years have passed,
without a word.

Years have passed,
Unseen, without a nuance.

Now, to see her in line – wishing for
deaf ears, a silent *hello*.

Dandle

Dark and light,
we're eye to eye,
a blinding fortress.

The winds blow -
Listen to trees whispering?
Stilts are tipping over.

Earthquake shakes, muscle and bones.
Inside out, where blood and skin
meet—string me,
marionette me.

I'm holding steady in wrinkled skin,
old and peeling.
Control me.

On

Nails dig into my back.

You bite my neck,
I'm dripping wet.

Turn me on with your slightest touch.
Your wet lips,
Between thighs and tongue.

Fall Victim

Soft, let these petals run.
Winds blow east to west,
whirlwind strong—
stay ahold, love.
We'll make it through,
outside without a wall—

we won't survive this wind,
unless these petals run.

Let
    these
        petals
            run,
                run,
                    run

 away.

Without catch,
without hold—
let me go.

Closed Eyes

It's not safe with you;
you lose everything.
Nonetheless, we share
the pills, that green small
affection.
As we lie
in a dark room,
walls crumble,
I fumble,
and I know it's not safe to stay.

Still, I take the chance,
Filling my void, for emotion,
Losing myself to feel something.

I **will** play this part.

Living Room Screening

The room is dark and we're not alone.
You touch my hand, smile quirkily.

I keep my distance, inches away—
what is it that you want?
When she leaves the room,
you tell me to stay.

I can't.

Though, we talk the night away over
airwaves.

Sunday Pride

Buttons pushed high, level red,
I threw out a feeling.

But, your arms were too busy
on someone else.

When It Rains, It Pours

The rain of the clouds slowly fall to the
ground.
I'm sitting on wooden benches
listening to the sounds.

The trees, I watch
as they sway and move
with the siren winds.

Fallen leaves
turn from green to gold
ending in dust.

I am not afraid to swim this storm,
to face the floods before me.

I've been swimming
before my feet learned to walk.

I can't give in to this tsunami.
I can't give up on you.
It's my only survival.

Noche

Quarter till midnight—the night
is still young. Your eyes are swollen
with midnight blues,
with-in minutes,
you've gone to another.

I know this feeling,
the wanting.

So, I'll be here in the morning,
hoping for your safe return.

disgusted.

Compatibility Mate

These notes play
a soft tune
behind closed
doors.

Windows
left open,
breeze winding
through.

Curtains
flow and catch
the night.

Hell's not
freezing the keys,
but we are dying
in this house.

Our last night
and the neighbors know.

Your bloody voice - my face flooded.

Your screams,
vibrate the walls
and the world knows,
this is our end.

The Walk Away

You're like those people who claim
all they want is love, following cheap
emotion;
on street corners where you lie to my
face, said there was nowhere else
for you to go.

The next night, you read your lines,
practiced your cries,
recited your fall.

There's only so long I can save you—

now my back has turned against you,
you're moving slowly.
As you decipher your next move,

I flee.

Pink Ocean

You let me see all
of the above, but below
is where I need to be,
without the glow of others.

False Profits

If I wrote you a story
would you live by the book?
If men wrote instead,
would you believe their words?

Once, I sat you down, and you didn't
follow the pattern. Would you know
who you were without the word's?
of those you'll never know?

Auction

Your playful manner in a glance,
a look, a smile, a touch, a feel.

I threw out a hint, a gesture, a tone as
stern as a *yes* with an under-
breathing breath.
Notice the gestures, my eyes, these
thoughts.
When the day comes to an end,
I'll no longer be there,
these exceptions silence knows.

By then I'll be over you.
Catch it fast!
I won't last on this line for too long,
Not for you!

Scars

Here we go again,
washing the blood off our faces.

It's going to be a long night.

As she is a wolf at our door, we'll fight,
So *"We let her in"*.

Teeth bite skin and we're bleeding
Freshly wounds.

Don't let us lose tonight?
Underground,
believing we know what's right.

Seasons

Winter knows the cold
as well I knew her.

Spring came to make amends
when she realized her mistake.

Summer held her own in a heated
argument
and knew when to leave.

Autumn—as much as the times
changed—
autumn knew to set me free.

Family traits

pour like a sin,
heal faster when
I'm stuck within
my own self—
the part that
you destroyed
long ago.
It still
tastes like sin.

Redolent

Beauty rush, a stranger's touch,
and I'm nowhere to be found.
Thoughts are running, soaking my liver.
Clothes come off and right back on.
Now I'm humming to a beat—one
that's not new to me.

It's a different tune, a farewell melody
untouchable. I'm falling slowly
into beds where I'd rather not sleep.

Laced-in eyes, quiet drive,
smoking cigarettes to keep me alive.
Wrapped in skin, I'm falling fast.

Taste of tongue in bed where I try
to manifest sleep.

The night is young,
 I, alive with it.

Where Have You Gone

Sorrows, struggles, dreams are spoiled.
Nightmares come and go.
Life's not easy, when madness
controls our souls.
Life is not a place for play; life is
where
I need to pay.

Though, it I open this door
to my heart, I can't fall in love with a
soul.

Mother, why would you abandon me?

I was just twelve years old—
I needed you.

Excuse

I no longer have to hurt.
If I'm too heavy for you to handle,
let me go!

You never took the chance
to carry me anyways.

The Door

Dark befriended me
again, uninvitingly.
I unlocked the bolts
willingly.

Give me a chance

To love you through
the mist and fog
of early morning
desire.

Impulsive

Skies darken to a different shade of
blue.
The wind is winding away from
familiar
faces. I'm not with you.

It's for the best, some will say.
Sun escapes moon and feelings get
lost
in translation.

What is with us?

Memories escape into my reality.
Are we in love?
You're not with me and I'm
not ready to move.

The Path of No Return

Growing up, drunk, I discovered
writing, and now
I know where to find myself
in that darkest hour.

Can in hand. Smoke in lungs.
Light of sativa.

Am I
an addict?

Decide.

Printed Forearm

I once had a rabbit
as black as hell's door,
a grandfather's gift before hell
and heavens made a choice.

Wings clipped so tight—
in time and endings.

I packed my darkness, my plastic-bag
home,
with an ending roar.
My dried eyes,
if only they'd tear for you.
There's no replacement.

I drove with your gift
inked on my arm with your name.

Distance left.

Three-hundred and twenty-two miles—

.

Hypersexuality

How I want to be on the other side
of the bed for once, instead of
tiptoeing
around the room.

Ready?

When your past is against us
and your future sometimes loses us—
what are we but two figures behind
closed curtains?
I've given up names,
given up space.
Your freckled face,
my freckled lips.
Pills feed our hunger
to not feel alone.

We are fucked up.

Blackened eyes, noir souls.
If this is a game,
let's see who wins in the end?

With friends we'll call truce anyway.

Floral Scent

He raised his voice
so loud that she heard
a crack, as the violinist
strung her strings,
the strings withered.

He swallowed
more pride than
the farmer when he knew his apples,
won blue ribbon at the state fair.

He—wait, he—
who knows how
to make a stand, when undressed,
revealed a woman with
the strength of a man.

Manic Depressive

She comes over me; I come over me.
Slithering from inside to my outer
skins,
she takes hold.
We birthed at the same hour,
same day—I can't be found.

I'm crying inside,
Outside fake laughter.
I'm a mistake, unforgivable, non-
spousal.

Could you forget and forgive me?
I'm holding this against me.

The Other Woman

I came around over
and over again, surrounded
by sex and cheap perfume.
Captured red lights where
I'm left alone in a crowded room.

Delicate

Violently, I heard her cry,
asking for one more try.

Daggers for words, she's killing
her only chance to stay; safe inside my
room.
Dark beside my bed, your love is the
killer,
Leading me to my death bed.

while you're numb,
I gave up breath to have you go.

I caused this.

Charmed lovers
outside our home.

I walked away
bold-legged,
turned the knob on our hidden floor,
next to my bed.

— I left with a splinter.

Cold and Blue

Tell me you hear me
from below the surface
even though you found
your way back
to that shallow place
where you lost me.

Painted skies, blue ribbon
tied around my neck.
Twist and turn, rewind your face
to replace the safe.

I'm on borrowed lungs
to replace the breath
I gave up so easily for you.
I'm a beaten scene—
down the path I'm walking free.

Comfort me down blue.
High tides will rise up soon,
slowly drowning me to where I belong,
underneath the eclipse of the moon.

Golden Tulips

I wish for so many things and I wish
for nothing at all.
I wish that's all it was. I wish more than
what I wish for,
Is to not wish at all.

Against a Name

Walked over and over
'til I slept ashore. The rainy
floods of my semblance
lost face; I've done this
before. We've borrowed lungs.
Easy enough to give up breath,
I inhaled your tongue,
without my own strength.

I'll bleed blue alone
when you're gone.
I know my worth;
I know you're lost.

Why are we still?

Countdown 3,2,1
Gone.

Give In

Before I went to sleep and the world
around me knew my fear,
I thought of you lying alone in a dark
room.
My wrist hit the floor, and no one
knew death was a heartbreak.
Failing to breathe, my chest sinks 'til
it's free.

Ideation

Happy thoughts, happy
thoughts, die
tonight, quietly.

ƐΝƬΡ

Known knowns
are the scariest. You know
it's there and you're still
puzzled?

There's only
one word for that:
love.

Seeing Red

I'll be your smoking gun,
falling down the barrel.

In the heat of the night
of revelry,
love,
this is a killing spree.

Same Speech

This feeling nauseates.
How much longer
can this go on?

I heard your cries,
your threats.

That drink in your hand leaves a car
crash calling,
But; you ignore the fact,
that this is the last time I give in - to my
oblivion.

Slippery Slopes

If I had the right words
to help you feel okay—here
I am, trying. I would tell you
in all the right ways,
what I need to say,
in words; I can't find meaning.
Show me the way.
I'm crimson bleeding.

Don't Bother

…And you're the only one that's
scared?
Spare me the details, if they were true.

Glue. Gun. Eyes.

Even in a sliver of light,
you'll only still be
a hidden shadow.

A silhouette in a memory—
a *warmth* I can never replace.

Water Sign

You're not a fish,
for you walk
on land, my dear.

Bottom of the Bottle

I'm back at the place
where the lights are dim;
the weather is storm,
my sight is blind.

Let go the feeling.

Build me from disaster,
I can't make a move
because without you
I am nothing.

Digital World

Wonders to be hated,
figurines set a new standard,
to that hallowed place
where the war took place.

Mind erasers
find erasers—
white erasers—
blank the pages,
where in history
bloodshed stains.

Though through eyes
you can't find the place,
in hearts you'll find
their pain,
with tears—
men,
women,
children,
erased.

Forgive the forsaken, for they
have been replaced.

Balderdash

I've listened on repeat for hours now
and I still feel the same
as yesterday. The more I listen,
the more I read between your lines,
of a great love song and a scribbled
name.

We both feel the same,
running in opposite directions.
Us and our cold war, us
and our heated skin.

Tell me we can hold this fear together -
without release.

III

In the midst of my nightmares, no one
could tell by only a look
that my sickness might prevail.
I have a faith that soon may blind me,
though never leave me in sight, as in
mind, where I'm prepared in muscle
and bone.

That in the end,
        I'll still be standing.

Roommate

She said, watery eyes, she wants me
back. I told her I never left.

She said you've been gone, this isn't my
home - I'm just living in it.
I looked away, shocked by all my
buildings, everything!

I've known this whole time,
blinding eyes.

In Soil

Even succulents die with
me.

How don't I see?
I am surrounded
by ivy.

Inside This Memory

I feel I've let you
down. Am wandering
again.

Win this battle
for me? Be my shield
and not melt
under pressure?

If you could,
Would you fight?
Would you last?
Would you win?

And if you couldn't, would you be
there; to listen to my final breath
as the fans' roar soars?

Apartment 203, Under Construction

I.
Come home and let's
leave this behind,
act like we were meant to be.
Here, we can build our fantasies.
Inside this book we'll mark our place.

II.
I know I made mistakes.
I couldn't guide you.
You were too new to this place.

III.
Tell me it's my fault.
Fist to my face
on a balcony of spectators,
yells/screams/tears.

IV.
And if you had told me,
would it be different?
Would we be magical?

Erica Varela

If you had told me,
would I still run away?
Baby, now you got me looking bad.
Baby, now you got me looking worse.

Light Switches

Carelessly, you undressed me.
I thought mute was our best way
as we slept naked in your bed.
Those beige and red sheets
may never be revisited again,
and all these things left unsaid
were carelessly swallowed.
Kept this tongue at rest
but couldn't stop the mind:

Carelessly I'm clearless.
Carelessly clearless.
Carelessly I drowned
in your bed.
Carelessly we swallowed too much lead.
Carelessly drowning in your bed.
Again, again, again, and again,
carelessly I drowned
in your bed again.

Not a fan of who you've become,
I sat on the finish line at the end of
your game.
Waited there to give myself back my
own name.

Closed Windows

I'm not good at this, the person
I wish to be. Find it easier to fade
away
in my own misery.

Erica Varela

Loyalty

Time and time has passed.
You call, I call.
Nostalgia breaks.
Time turns to years,
speeds by.

Time restrains you
in a white bed. I'm on my way
to remove you
from harm's way.

Autumn

From the trees, leaves crumble,
winds fumble. She whispers
to not make a sound. Not a peep.
Light touch, shy hold.
Die with the sun.
Moon brings out your touch
and I make a move.

I'm in the *nude*.

Cracked Glass Lips

How I've learned
from your falsifying
tongue.

Shatter us—
leave me with scars.

unbeknown,
simple patterns
I know.

Broken cuts.

Death

Ma vie de la poésie est faite de
velours—
my life of poetry is made of velvet.

Can't Express

I walked away, took the low
Rhode, where the cement turned to
ambling dirt.
That was my biggest mistake.
I gave you my past; you still went along
for the ride
without me at the wheel.

When we were alone, my mind was
always elsewhere;
and that's not how I feel,
but; I let my mind do the thinking.
If my heart were big enough, I would
not
have left, would not have let you go.

Fourth Letter of the Alphabet

I would call her selfish, absorbed, a
looker of likes.
May I not lower myself, a mantra.

Maturity

The room says it all—
tins crunching, scraping
metals.
Our ears ring
or teeth vibrate.

Aside from what I know,
I knew it was our last night—
that jump forward
gave a purpose.
Vocally, this wall
will not decrease,
not even surrender.
Maybe I'll tell you in time,
when your face shows
your age, how to surrender.

White Pills

Looked in the mirror to see
a reflection, stared 'til eyes dried
without a blink. No movement.

Held on
strong and still.
I said,
just take me, I can't do this
anymore.

My face, smeared
and wiped to perfection.

You're only as heavy as a shadow
that only comes out on a sunny day,
but it's dark where I am and without
the sun,
I can't find you.
Mirror in hand, facing my face,
white pill find me.

Selfish Human Me

Shelter me in a forest
and I will run free.
Hide me behind your sheets,
I will give in.
Hand me your heart,
I'll try to keep it safe
as long as mine is still beating.

Drained

She'll write you a story,
make an ending for you.
You'll have to take that chance.

Believe what she says,
what she does, though
it's all in her head.

She wants out, is stuck
in her body, talks through her veins.
Watch me now, learning by
mistakes.
Take my place.
Refill my veins.

Mixed State

I woke up; I fell again.
I woke up; I fell again.
I woke up; I woke up
just to fall again.

Bivouac

You left the comfortable world—a
woman
took you by the hand. She fought the
black shadows,
you on your deathbed. The devil's son
through the heavens and closed doors
comforted you, took care of you.
Soon you'll forget about everything,
including
your disease. Blackened lungs. Shady,
swollen face.
You don't deserve the light of the sun
or the moon, only a coffin below soil
where weeds grow. All the shaved trees
burn bright.
You'll lament that you had everything
in life.
Get comfortable here, where you will
never
feel love again.

Vibrating Lungs

Hear that sound, that echo?
That's the sound we make,
you and I. Give me some motion.

Give me a leap to another place
in time, where we find each other
in painful visions. Slit throat.

This new bed for sleep, different
sheets.
What happens when we can't hear
our sound anymore?

Debris

I want you more than the river's edge.
You kept me wet enough to live on the
crest,
but it's drying out here
and love is at its end.
My thoughts have nowhere to go.

Find a place to set them free—

My tongue is wrapped around
other lips, not as sweet
as I believed them to be. Lying on the
river's
edge, I'm dried inside.
The river's peak,
keep me wet enough
to learn how to breathe.

Rewinding

I let you in my world slowly.
Time passes; these batteries I keep
near
need to recharge. This time you're by
my side.
Tell me for how long, because I
remember
before: white walls and a sinner's body,
dead of the night, stars still shinning.
Watery eyes, your words spill out over
wet lips—
the sun is rising, brighter as my
departure
nears. This time say you'll stay,
show yourself. As long as you love me
we can press *play*.

Sueno

I remember going places,
taking chances on the midnight train,
discovering voices racing in the rain.

Earthquakes shook the ground we
walked on
'til our soles were sore. Birds falling
from trees—
I remember making love on the sand,
your hair blowing in the wind.
The strangers got a view, and we
noticed,
laughed, ran somewhere new.

I woke up to the smell of your taste
on my lips, stained like wine.

I remember the boat ride—you by my
side

as we set sail. That island, our escape.
I remember all that we meant
to each other, that time.

ABOUT THE AUTHOR

Golden Honey is Erica Varela's second book, following *Set Free*. Varela was born and raised in Perth Amboy, NJ and now resides in Los Angeles, CA. She has been writing poetry for over twenty years and still continues to follow her passion, as well many other professions—she also works for one of the largest music labels in the world for over a decade.

COMING SOON

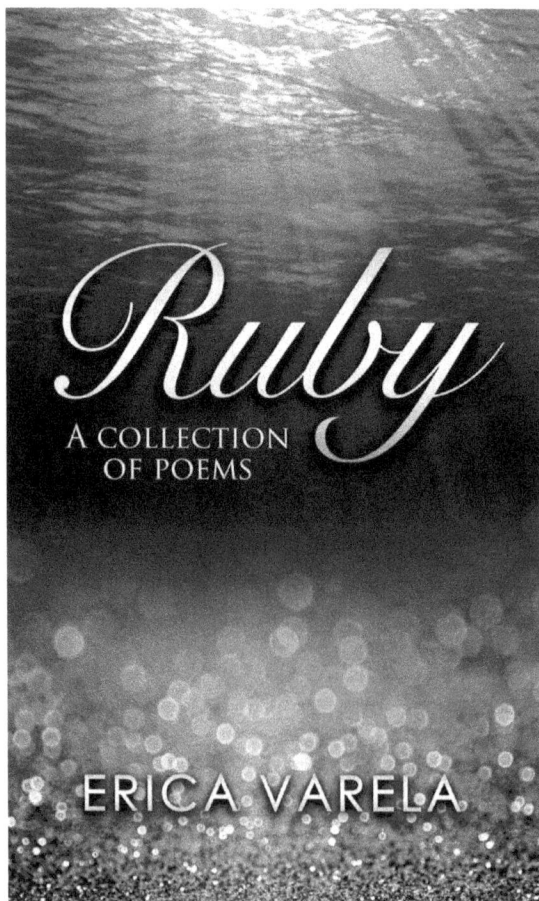

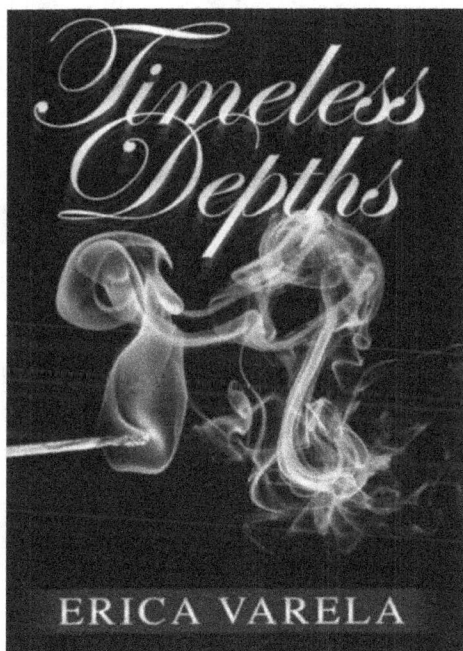

CARLOS MEDINA
THE
Phases
OF THE
Soul

MAGESOUL
PUBLISHING

WWW.MAGESOUL.COM

PRECIOUS PAIN
The Spirit's Destiny

Carlos Medina

MAGESOUL
PUBLISHING

WWW.MAGESOUL.COM

AVAILABLE

JULY 2019

CARLOS MEDINA

Seeking

THE UNKNOWN

WWW.MAGESOUL.COM

AUTHORS:
Myke Duarte Carlos
Carlos Medina

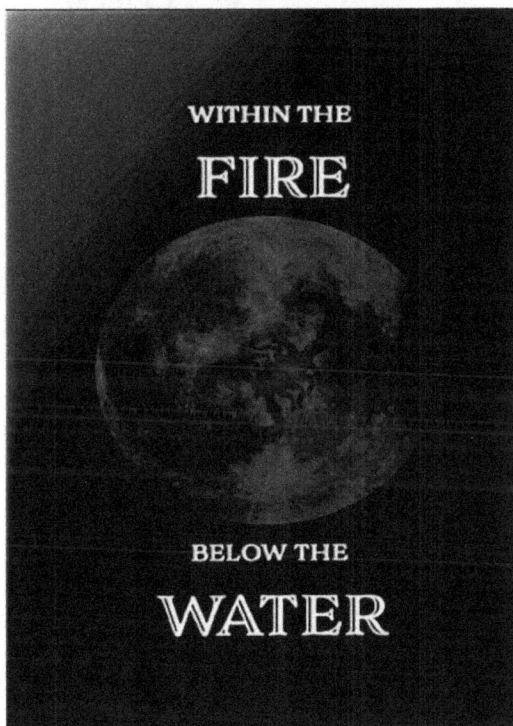

WITHIN THE

FIRE

BELOW THE

WATER

AVAILABLE

WWW.MAGESOUL.COM

Erica Varela

Salted
Caramel Tears

by Natalie White

"The Soul speaks a language.
that words often fail to articulate.
I try anyway"

Come on a journey of healing
within Natalie's debut collection.
"Salted Caramel Tears"
as she carries you through
four chapters of Loss. Lessons. Love.
the final destination. Light.

COMING SUMMER 2019

www.magesoul.com

Magesoul Publishing is now accepting
submissions from writers in the future who wish
to get their book published through this
corporation.

Submit or send inquiries to:
submissions@magesoulpublishing.com